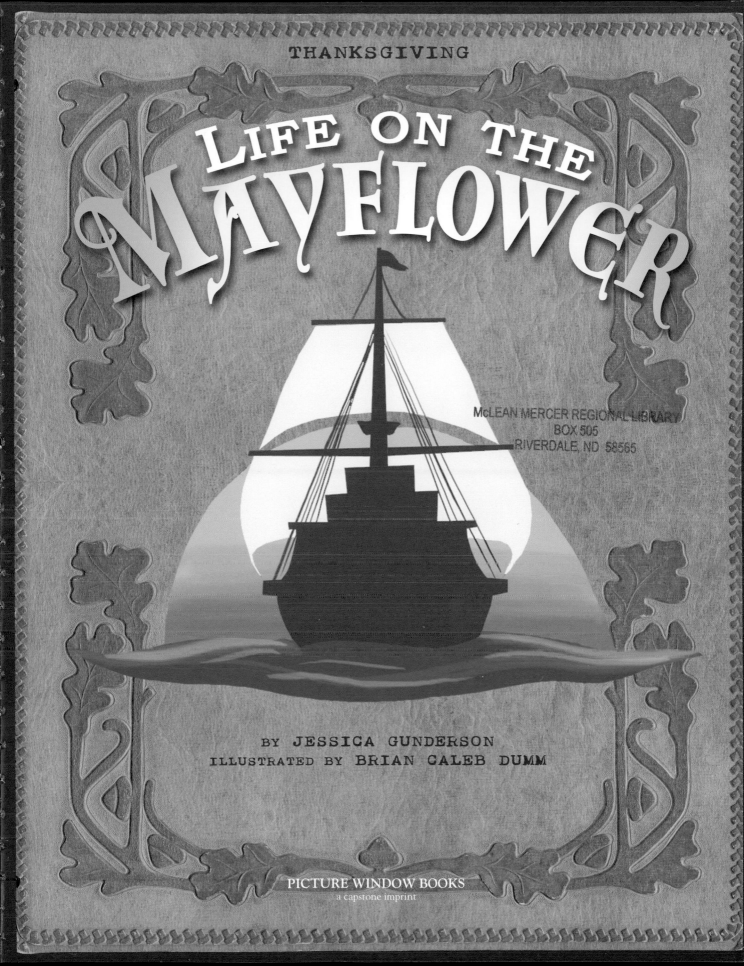

THANKSGIVING

Life on the
Mayflower

BY JESSICA GUNDERSON
ILLUSTRATED BY BRIAN CALEB DUMM

PICTURE WINDOW BOOKS
a capstone imprint

On a windy September day in 1620, a ship called the *Mayflower* set sail from the coast of England. On board, families huddled together. Children peered around their parents for a last look at the land they were leaving behind. Then, excitedly, they turned their faces to the sea. Ahead was a new life and a new land—America.

3

The *Mayflower* usually carried goods such as wine and cloth. But on this journey, passengers were her cargo. The *Mayflower* carried 102 passengers and about 25 crew members. It also held two dogs, some goats, chickens, and other animals.

Many of the passengers were Separatists, members of a religious group that had split from the Church of England. In the early 1600s, English law said that everyone had to follow the Church of England. Many Separatists, later called Pilgrims, moved to the Netherlands, where they could worship freely.

The Pilgrims had been living in the Netherlands for 12 years, but they longed for their own community. They decided to start a colony in America.

The first week at sea, the weather was calm and warm. Children ran above deck. But soon, autumn winds began to blow, tossing the Mayflower around. The passengers were not used to the sea rolling beneath them. Many got sick and had to stay on the lower deck. Some of the crew made fun of the passengers' seasickness.

The lower deck became the passengers' home away from home. Animals rode there too. It was dark and damp. The ceiling was so low that many adults could not stand up straight. There were no windows. Lanterns supplied the only light.

In the cramped space, children had no room to run.
To pass the time, they probably sang or read the Bible.
They may have played board games such as Nine
Men's Morris, which is like checkers.

With no way to keep food cold on the ship, passengers had to bring food that wouldn't spoil. They ate salted meat, dried peas, hard biscuits, cheese, and oatmeal. With few places on board to cook, passengers made large kettles of stew for everyone to share.

There was no bathroom on the *Mayflower*. People
used small pots and emptied them into the ocean.
There also wasn't much water for washing. The
lower deck and the cargo hold below stank. And
the air grew more sour with each passing day.

Out in the Atlantic Ocean, storms could be so strong and loud it seemed like the ship would break apart. One night, terrible winds cracked a wooden beam that supported the ship's frame. Without it, the ship could not sail. Everyone worried the ship would have to return to England. Even some crew members thought the *Mayflower* was doomed.

Luckily, one of the passengers had a large iron screw to
hold the beam in place. Once fixed, the ship sailed on.

Another storm threatened the life of a passenger named John Howland. John was above deck when the storm broke. Without warning, strong winds and rain swept him into the ocean. He called for help. No one on board knew what to do.

Then, when all hope seemed lost, John grabbed one of the ship's ropes. Several crew members pulled him back onto the ship. He was wet and cold, but he was safe.

On November 9, after 65 days at sea, the *Mayflower* crew spotted land. But the journey wasn't over yet. The *Mayflower* anchored in Cape Cod while a small group explored the coast.

Native Americans called the Wampanoag were already living there. Unsure of one another, the Wampanoag and the Pilgrims kept their distance.

18

The Pilgrims learned of an empty village nearby called Patuxet. There they started building their houses. They worked on them by day and slept on the ship at night. The Pilgrims renamed the village Plymouth.

Finally, after almost three months, there were enough homes for everyone. On April 5, the *Mayflower* set sail for England. And a new life began in America for her former passengers.

Timeline of Key Dates

June 1619
The Pilgrims gain permission from the Virginia Company to set up a colony.

September 6, 1620
The *Mayflower* sets sail from Plymouth, England.

November 9, 1620
Land is sighted.

November 11, 1620
The *Mayflower* anchors in Cape Cod. The men sign the Mayflower Compact, an agreement between the passengers to set up a new community.

December 20, 1620
The Pilgrims settle in Patuxet and rename it Plymouth. The Wampanoag had lived there until a few years before, when sickness destroyed most of the village.

December 23, 1620
The Pilgrims begin building.

March 16, 1621
An Abenaki Native American from Maine named Samoset walks into the village. He welcomes the settlers in English. He had learned to speak it from traders he'd met.

March 22, 1621
The Pilgrims sign a peace treaty with Massasoit, a leader of the Wampanoag people. The Wampanoag had lived in the area for thousands of years.

April 5, 1621
The *Mayflower* returns to England with the crew.

Strange But True

On the *Mayflower*, everyone drank beer, even the children. Water was not considered safe to drink.

One baby was born on the journey. The baby was named Oceanus.

Not all *Mayflower* passengers were Separatists. Some were moving to America to better their lives, not for religious freedom. They were later known as "Strangers."

The English the *Mayflower* passengers spoke was a bit different than today's English. Instead of saying, "How are you?" a passenger may have said, "Good day" or "What cheer?" Instead of saying, "Goodbye," he or she may have said, "Fare thee well."

Glossary

anchor—to hold in place with something heavy

cargo—goods carried by ship, airplane, or truck

colony—a place settled by people from another country that follows that country's laws

Pilgrim—one of the people who came to America in 1620 for religious freedom and set up Plymouth Colony; a pilgrim is also someone who goes on a religious journey

Separatist—a member of a religious group that split from the Church of England in the 1600s

spoil—to rot

worship—to pray

Read More

Lassieur, Allison. *The Voyage of the Mayflower.* Graphic Library: Graphic History. Mankato, Minn.: Capstone Press, 2006.

Philbrick, Nathaniel. *The Mayflower and the Pilgrims' New World.* New York: G.P. Putnam's Sons, 2008.

Plimoth Plantation, with Peter Arenstam, John Kemp, and Catherine O'Neill Grace. *Mayflower 1620: A New Look at a Pilgrim Voyage.* Washington, D.C.: National Geographic, 2003.

Internet Sites

FactHound offers a safe, fun way to find Internet sites related to this book. All of the sites on FactHound have been researched by our staff.

Here's all you do:

Visit *www.facthound.com*

Type in this code: 9781404862845

Super-cool stuff! Check out projects, games and lots more at www.capstonekids.com

Look for all the books in the Thanksgiving series:

Life on the Mayflower
The Pilgrims' First Thanksgiving
Thanksgiving Crafts
Thanksgiving Recipes
Thanksgiving Then and Now

Index

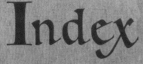

Special thanks to our advisers for their expertise:

Plimoth Plantation
Plymouth, Massachusetts

Terry Flaherty, PhD, Professor of English
Minnesota State University, Mankato

Editor: Jill Kalz
Designer: Alison Thiele
Art Director: Nathan Gassman
Production Specialist: Michelle Biedscheid
The illustrations in this book were created digitally.

Photo Credits: Shutterstock/Lou Oates, 1, 21, 22,
23, 24 (background texture); Worldpics, throughout,
(typewriter key)

Picture Window Books
151 Good Counsel Drive
P.O. Box 669
Mankato, MN 56002-0669
877-845-8392
www.capstonepub.com

Library of Congress Cataloging-in-Publication Data
Gunderson, Jessica.
  Life on the Mayflower / by Jessica Gunderson ; illustrated by
Brian Caleb Dumm.
     p. cm. — (Thanksgiving)
  Includes index.
  ISBN 978-1-4048-6284-5 (library binding)
  ISBN 978-1-4048-6719-2 (paperback)
  1. Pilgrims (New Plymouth Colony)—Juvenile literature.
  2. Mayflower (Ship)—Juvenile literature. 3. Massachusetts—
History—New Plymouth, 1620-1691—Juvenile literature.
  I. Title.
  F68.G886 2011
  974.4'02—dc22   2010033762

Printed in the United States of America in North Mankato,
Minnesota.   092010   005933CGS11

A DOZEN SILK DIAPERS

Melissa Kajpust

Illustrated by Veselina Tomova

Hyperion Books for Children
New York

FIRST EDITION
1 3 5 7 9 10 8 6 4 2

Library of Congress Cataloging-in-Publication Data
Kajpust, Melissa.
A dozen silk diapers/Melissa Kajpust: illustrated by Veselina Tomova – 1st ed.
p.   cm.
Summary: A mother spider and her children, who live in the manger
in Bethlehem where Jesus is born, make a simple but loving
gift for him.
ISBN 1-56282-456-2 (trade) – ISBN 1-56282-457-0 (lib. bdg.)
1. Jesus Christ – Juvenile fiction. [1. Jesus Christ – Nativity – Fiction.
2. Spiders – Fiction.] I. Tomova, Veselina, ill. II. Title.
PZ7.K123445Do   1993
92-41937
[E] – dc20   CIP   AC

The illustrations are prepared with watercolor.
This book is set in 20-point Garamond.

For Daniel, Holly, and David

A long time ago, a mother spider
lived with her forty tiny children
in a stable outside Bethlehem.

The mother spider was gentle and loving.
Her many children kept her busy, yet she was
always willing to help others if they needed
her. When the lamb broke its leg, the mother
spider spun a web round and round to form
a strong and sturdy cast.

When the roof leaked directly over the donkey's stall, the mother spider plugged the hole with mud and grass that she joined with silk threads. All the animals appreciated her special care.

One evening a brilliant star lit up the sky and shone directly over the stable. "What does it mean?" the little spiders asked their mother.

"I don't know," she replied, "but surely it must signify something wonderful."

8

That same evening a young woman named Mary came to the stable. She and her husband, Joseph, sought shelter because they could find no other place.

Soon Mary gave birth to a baby boy and called him Jesus. The spiders and the other animals watched quietly as the young mother wrapped the child in soft blankets and laid him in a manger filled with straw.

The little spiders wanted to visit the new baby as they had visited all the other new babies that were born in the stable. The mother spider forbade them. "You may frighten the baby and his mother," she said. "Most people don't like spiders, and some harm may come to you." Grudgingly her children crawled back to their nest under the cattle trough.

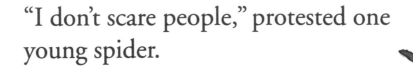

"I don't scare people," protested one young spider.

Cautiously he crawled out of the nest, past his sleeping brothers and sisters, determined to see the new child.

He moved quickly up the wall and along the rafter and stopped directly over the manger, where the baby lay sleeping, tended by Mary.

The little spider could not see clearly from
his position, so he moved closer to the edge.
He stretched his eight skinny legs out as far
as he could until his tiny knobby knees began
to quiver and his small round furry body
began to shake.

When he stretched again he could no longer
hold on. Down he fell, right into the manger,
beside the sleeping baby. When he opened his
eyes and shook the dizziness out of his head,
he saw that Mary was peering down at him.

He heard her easy laughter. She reached into the manger, carefully scooped him up in her hand, and told him to scurry home. The mother spider was annoyed with her child and scolded him for not obeying her.

The little spider was on his way back to bed when he saw three men in flowing robes enter the stable. They had come to visit Mary and had brought rich gifts for the baby.

The little spider asked, "Can we give the baby a present, too?"

"I'm grateful for the woman's kindness, but what shall we give?" his mother replied sadly. "We have nothing."

Suddenly she had an idea! She awakened all her children and gathered them around her to tell them her plan.

Far into the night, while her children spun silk, the mother spider wove all the threads together. They finished just as the sun's rays stretched over the horizon.

A dozen silk diapers glimmered in the early
morning light. The mother spider folded
them carefully and asked the lamb to help
move them to where the baby and his
mother slept.

When Mary awoke she was delighted with the gift. She thought they were the most beautiful diapers she had ever seen. But from where did they come? By chance she looked up to the rafter, where she saw the mother spider and all her children watching her. Then she remembered the little spider. "Thank you," she said. "You have made a lovely gift for my baby. Please, come closer and see him."

The spiders gathered along the edge of
the manger to gaze at the sleeping child.
The adventuresome young spider, however,
climbed up the wall beside the manger
and sat on the edge of the small window
for his glimpse of the baby.

A long shaft of light touched the corner of the stall where the rich gifts were placed. The little spider saw the gold and jewels and sweet-scented spices. But now in the very center were the shimmering silk diapers.